ENCOUNTER

God

JOURNAL

ERIKA JANE BAKER

ISBN: 978109026214

Published by Amazon.c

Dedication

To You Daddy,
in hopes that others can also Encounter You.

To my kids,
Liam, Paisley & Silas -
I pray that you might Encounter your Father
in Heaven, Your Daddy even more than your
Earthly Father and I have. You are amazing
kids and I know He has BIG plans for you.

For those who want to desperately
Encounter God, hear from Him and be able
to recall all of the times He showed up for
you and those you know,

This is for you.

PS. NONE of this would be possible without my husband, Bryan, and his
constant showing of our Father's love, patience and support of me - it
fuels me everyday. Love you babe.

0   HOW TO USE THIS JOURNAL

1   JOURNALING

33   SERMONS

65   DREAMS

97   PROPHETIC WORDS

129   PRAYERS

161   HEARING GOD MAP

169   SIGNS & SYMBOLS

201   WORDS HEARD

231   OPEN & CLOSED DOORS

265   VISIONS & PICTURES

297   MIRACLES

TABLE OF contents

How to use this journal

There are two parts to this journal. The 10 different major ways you can hear God:

Through Journaling. Sermons. Dreams. Prophetic Words. Prayers. Signs & Symbols. Words Heard. Open & Closed Doors. Miracles. Visions & Pictures. and then Mapping all of these Encounters by using the Hearing God Map in this journal.

This is not an all inclusive list but it will help group the major ways you can hear God. If you are first starting out, you might think you only hear from Him in 1 or maybe not even any ways. That's okay. That's where I was 5 years ago until someone pointed out that He was talking to me - I just wasn't recognizing it.

The point of having all of these sections is to EXPECT that God will show up in some if not all of these ways to talk to you. Sometimes you will even go through seasons where He tends to talk to you in one way more than the other - and that's totally normal! (Again - I'm not saying I know everything but I do know how He is has talked to me and those around me!)

As we have these encounters, sometimes we forget to write the stories down or we do and can't find them to reference amongst the piles of journals we have.

That's why I created this journal. So you can visually map by theme, your Encounters with God and see the different ways He speaks to you about similar themed things over the years.

By using the map that starts on page 161 - you will be able to keep track of your encounters and be able to quickly reference them when talking to a friend, small group, missional community or family member about how God is showing up in your life.

God gave me a vision as I was creating this book. A vision of the impact of being able to hand a completely filled journal to your child or friend - who is exploring their faith journey with God and allowing them to see how our amazing Dad showed up for us so they can understand the way we Encounter Him on a daily basis. Could you imagine if someone did that to us? How much more quickly we could recognize what encountering God in today's world looks like? And how we could understand His heart even more? It would be amazing.

Journaling

This is one of my FAVORITE ways of talking to God lately but I HATE writing long things. Yes you heard me. The cool thing is, is that lately, because I've been allowing my thoughts that seem to "randomly" pop into my head as I journal, to be considered as things to note and check with God to see if they are from Him - I've been able to see Him move so much. Not just in my life but in those around me.

I have been able to have conversations with God by just journaling back and forth with Him. I know it sounds a bit odd - and it takes some tuning your ear into when you see that something you heard was clearly from Him and aligns with scripture and those things that were of your own thoughts.

I always check what I think I hear with what the Bible says to see if it's congruent with what God's character is and what He has said to us in the past.

Honestly, journaling and praying can sometimes seem like same thing when you approach journaling this way. All I ask if that you expect God to show up. I have never been disappointed. So whatever journaling might look like for you, don't be afraid of it - just write and see how he shows up for you! He wants nothing more than relationship with you.

journaling

date:

journaling

date:

journaling

date:

journaling

date:

journaling

date:

journaling

date:

journaling

date:

journaling

journaling

date:

journaling

date:

journaling

date:

journaling

date:

journaling

date:

journaling

date:

journaling

date:

date:

journaling

date:

journaling

date:

journaling

date:

journaling

date:

journaling

date:

journaling

date:

journaling

date:

journaling

date:

journaling

date:

journaling

date:

journaling

date:

journaling

date:

journaling

date:

journaling

date:

Sermons

Through our pastor or pastors of other churches, God has spoken more than once to me. Sometimes it's the point of the sermon that has been brought up to me for the 800th time and I'm sitting there looking at God like, "Okay okay, I get it already Dad."

Then other times it will seemingly have nothing to do with the sermon but as I was listening a thought pops into my head. Sometimes it's a part of my to do list - and honestly, at first when I came back to God, that was a lot of my random thoughts. And that's okay. Jot it down somewhere so you wont forget and come back to concentrating on the sermon.

Now-a-days though, it's more of things that God seems to be stirring up. A name of a random person that I haven't talked to in over a year as we discuss reaching out and being community to those we live near.

In the past I would ignore these "coincidences" or random things I would think during sermons, but now, I write them all down. Feel free to do the same. Remember - you can't "fail" at this listening and hearing God thing. Just step into it and ask God to show up. He will.

date:

sermons

date:

sermons

date:

sermons

date:

date:

sermons

date:

sermons

date:

sermons

date:

sermons

date:

sermons

date:

date:

date:

sermons

date:

sermons

date:

date:

sermons

date:

date:

sermons

date:

sermons

date:

sermons

date:

date:

sermons

date:

date:

date:

sermons

date:

sermons

date:

sermons

date:

sermons

date:

sermons

date:

sermons

date:

sermons

date:

Dreams

Dreams. What is there to say about dreams. Man, I have had a TON of them. Especially lately. I used to always be a vivid dreamer but always thought that was normal for everyone. I never even thought they could possibly mean anything.

I don't know why I didn't think God could talk to me through dreams. I mean He talked to people in the Bible in dreams, so they couldn't He talk to me like that? I finally started realizing He was talking to me and He's probably talking to you too!

I have actually experienced some of my greatest healing through dreams but since I can't seem to interpret my dreams yet, I have a really good friend that I talk to about them. (Thanks Robyn!)

One of my most pivotal ones was when I had a dream about my house being torn down to the studs in a horrible tornado. Everyone was safe but the house was down to the studs and I was upset. But then in the dream, an older couple came into our house after and helped us see how all of the hard work of tearing down the old stuff had been done and cast vision for all of the new things that could from this craziness.

I had been battling my idea of what church planting "should" look like and I hated the outdated way of the strict condemning ways of the church and it was brought out that God was asking me to re-think the ways I was viewing our "house" (our church/ministry) and to allow Him to re-define what it should look like. I was a wreck. I had dismissed/rebelled against any idea of formal ministry. But just from this one dream - my heart was completely turned. #cuzGod

Lesson Learned: Write down your dreams. You'll thank me later.

dreams

date:

dreams

dreams

date:

dreams

date:

dreams

dreams

dreams

dreams

date:

dreams

dreams

dreams

date:

dreams

dreams

date:

dreams

date:

dreams

date:

dreams

date:

dreams

date:

dreams

date:

dreams

dreams

date:

dreams

date:

dreams

date:

dreams

date:

dreams

date:

dreams

date:

dreams

dreams

dreams

dreams

date:

dreams

date:

dreams

I didn't even know what a prophetic word was a few years ago. Thank goodness I do now. I feel like I missed out on half of my relationship with my Daddy (God) and the Holy Spirit.

If you have experience with Prophetic Words or not, it's totally fine. All experiences are welcome here. PS - Skeptics are always welcome. I was one before too because of the inauthenticity that this area can have. Don't worry, it can be authentic when done right so don't dismiss it yet.

For those starting or experienced in prophetic words, it is paramount to record these to remember them as well as check them with God for validity.

This can be a very exciting portion of your mapping of encounters with God and TOTALLY worth it.

prophetic words

date:

prophetic words

prophetic words

date:

prophetic words

date:

prophetic words

date:

prophetic words

date:

prophetic words

date:

prophetic words

date:

prophetic words

date:

prophetic words

prophetic words

date:

prophetic words

date:

prophetic words

date:

date:

prophetic words

date:

prophetic words

date:

prophetic words

date:

prophetic words

date:

prophetic words

date:

prophetic words

date:

prophetic words

date:

prophetic words

prophetic words

prophetic words

date:

prophetic words

date:

prophetic words

prophetic words

prophetic words

date:

prophetic words

date:

prophetic words

prophetic words

date:

Prayers

When praying to God, sometimes my mind wanders and it's hard to feel that He is actually there listening.

And honestly, having time to sit down and set everything aside for hours to pray seemed impossible with 3 kids under 5 years old. The cool thing I've experienced is that praying to our Father in Heaven, is that He doesn't ask us to be all formal and such. He asks us to be real with Him and to come to Him with EVERYTHING.

I worry less about my mess and being perfect and talk to Him like the unconditional loving Daddy that He is.

He is okay with our mess and interrupted thoughts. So I talk to Him rather than making it this big deal prayer thing. We talk ALL.DAY. LONG. In the car on my way to drop off the kids in the morning when I'm already exhausted and losing my patience. I also talk to Him while I listen to a song at work and I'm working on my next project and tell Him how thankful I am for my job.

Prayer is more of a constant dialogue than an occasional request sheet. He wants to know how we feel and be involved in a daily lives. He wants us to find rest and peace in Him and rely on Him to take care of us. Because He will!

Use these sheets to write down the prayers you pray during the day so you can track how God shows up when you pray for specific things.

prayers

date:

date answered:

prayers

date: _____

_____

_____

_____

_____

_____

_____

_____

_____

_____

_____

_____

_____

_____

_____

_____

_____

_____

_____

_____

_____

_____

_____

_____

_____

_____

_____

_____

_____

_____

_____

_____

_____

_____

prayers

date: _____ date answered: _____

prayers

date: date answered:

prayers

date: date answered:

prayers

date: date answered:

prayers

date: _____   date answered: _____

_____
_____
_____
_____
_____
_____
_____
_____
_____
_____
_____
_____
_____
_____
_____
_____
_____
_____
_____
_____
_____
_____
_____
_____
_____
_____
_____
_____
_____
_____
_____
_____
_____
_____
_____
_____
_____
_____

prayers

date: date answered:

prayers

date answered:

prayers

date: _____   date answered: _____

_____
_____
_____
_____
_____
_____
_____
_____
_____
_____
_____
_____
_____
_____
_____
_____
_____
_____
_____
_____
_____
_____
_____
_____
_____
_____
_____
_____
_____
_____
_____
_____
_____
_____
_____
_____

prayers

date: _____ date answered: _____

_____
_____
_____
_____
_____
_____
_____
_____
_____
_____
_____
_____
_____
_____
_____
_____
_____
_____
_____
_____
_____
_____
_____
_____
_____
_____
_____
_____
_____
_____
_____
_____
_____
_____
_____
_____
_____

prayers

date answered:

prayers

date:

date answered:

prayers

date: _____   date answered: _____

_____
_____
_____
_____
_____
_____
_____
_____
_____
_____
_____
_____
_____
_____
_____
_____
_____
_____
_____
_____
_____
_____
_____
_____
_____
_____
_____
_____
_____
_____
_____
_____
_____
_____
_____
_____
_____
_____
_____
_____
_____
_____
_____
_____
_____
_____

prayers

date: _____   date answered: _____

_____
_____
_____
_____
_____
_____
_____
_____
_____
_____
_____
_____
_____
_____
_____
_____
_____
_____
_____
_____
_____
_____
_____
_____
_____
_____
_____
_____
_____
_____
_____
_____
_____
_____
_____
_____
_____
_____
_____
_____

prayers

date: date answered:

prayers

date answered:

prayers

date: date answered:

prayers

date answered:

prayers

prayers

date: date answered:

prayers

date: _____ date answered: _____

prayers

date: _____   date answered: _____

prayers

date: date answered:

prayers

date: _____

_____
_____
_____
_____
_____
_____
_____
_____
_____
_____
_____
_____
_____
_____
_____
_____
_____
_____
_____
_____
_____
_____
_____
_____
_____
_____
_____
_____
_____
_____
_____
_____
_____
_____
_____
_____
_____
_____
_____
_____
_____
_____

prayers

date: date answered:

prayers

date: _____   date answered: _____

_____
_____
_____
_____
_____
_____
_____
_____
_____
_____
_____
_____
_____
_____
_____
_____
_____
_____
_____
_____
_____
_____
_____
_____
_____
_____
_____
_____
_____
_____
_____
_____
_____
_____
_____

prayers

date: _____   date answered: _____

_____
_____
_____
_____
_____
_____
_____
_____
_____
_____
_____
_____
_____
_____
_____
_____
_____
_____
_____
_____
_____
_____
_____
_____
_____
_____
_____
_____
_____
_____
_____
_____
_____
_____

prayers

date: _____   date answered: _____

_____
_____
_____
_____
_____
_____
_____
_____
_____
_____
_____
_____
_____
_____
_____
_____
_____
_____
_____
_____
_____
_____
_____
_____
_____
_____
_____
_____
_____
_____
_____
_____

prayers

date: date answered:

prayers

date: _____   date answered: _____

_____
_____
_____
_____
_____
_____
_____
_____
_____
_____
_____
_____
_____
_____
_____
_____
_____
_____
_____
_____
_____
_____
_____
_____
_____
_____
_____
_____
_____
_____
_____
_____
_____
_____
_____
_____

Hearing God Map

Here is the opportunity to connect the dots between the different things you hear from God whether that be through your dreams, a prophetic word you receive or from journaling to God and hearing something. All of these added together start to craft your story with God.

A lot of the times I catch myself forgetting little words or dreams that at the time didn't make sense but I wrote them down. Then while talking to someone they will randomly pop into my head as being applicable to that situation.

I used to think these were silly or just coincidences but now I'm starting to realize it isn't. It's just another way God is talking to me. Now because we have this journal that we can use to connect the dots, we can now add the page number of the Encounter with God, to a theme that God is working on in our lives.

I'll give you an example below to show you how you might use this section (it's how I use it!).

My goal for you is to be able to be talking to someone about what God has been doing and then be able to tell them the different encounters you had with God that are related to that topic. Then over the years you can see how God continues to speak to you about new things and old things. This will not only help your faith grow as you remember how you encountered God but it will also help grow the faith of those around you as you continue to share your stories.

PG 87 PG 218
MY IDENTITY
PG 10   PG 23

PG 41
BEING A
LEADER
PG 278   PG 95
PG 3

PG 37   PG 62
FEAR OF
FAILING
PG 215

Hearing God Map

A lot of the ways God has shown up with Signs & Symbols for me personally is through having something repeat over and over again as I go through my life. Maybe it is a song or a word or a number that I can feel in my gut after a while that it's significant but sometimes I'm not 100% sure why. Then at some later date I usually have more clarity around it.

Signs and Symbols can mean different things and happen differently for everybody because God talks to His kids differently based on their unique personalities and circumstances.

Just make sure to document whatever you feel might have significance and see how God shows up!

date:

signs & symbols

date:

date:

signs & symbols

date:

date:

signs & symbols

date:

date:

date:

date:

signs & symbols

date:

signs & symbols

date:

signs & symbols

date:

signs & symbols

date:

date:

date:

signs & symbols

date:

date:

date:

signs & symbols

date:

signs & symbols

date:

date:

signs & symbols

date:

date:

signs & symbols

signs & symbols

date:

signs & symbols

date:

date:

signs & symbols

date:

date:

signs & symbols

date:

date:

My whole life I would have random thoughts or words or phrases or people's names pop into my head. A lot of them were like, "Wow, where did that come from?" But now I'm starting to realize more and more that that's one of the ways God communicates with me - even when I was really young.

How do I know that? Because when I choose to step into those words or ideas or thoughts that seemingly drop into my head, big things happen, like a women breaking down because I asked her if the "her place by the lake" meant anything to her because I felt God wouldn't let me stop thinking about it when praying for her and when shared with her she said It was where she spent her time with God and recently felt like He had abandoned her.

Or hearing the word turtle while praying for a friend and thinking, "This is it, I've finally cracked." and it meaning the world to him because he has always considered himself a turtle and barricading himself in his shell and not letting others in and had recently felt like God was asking Him to step out of that.

Words heard can be a bunch of different things to you but I do know, a lot of things we dismiss as not valuable or silly can actually be God trying to tell us something that either impacts our lives or those around us. Don't ignore these. Write them down.

words heard

date:

words heard

date:

words heard

date:

date:

words heard

date:

words heard

date:

words heard

date:

words heard

date:

words heard

date:

words heard

date:

words heard

date:

words heard

date:

words heard

date:

date:

words heard

date:

words heard

date:

words heard

date:

words heard

date:

words heard

date:

date:

date:

date:

date:

words heard

date:

words heard

date:

date:

words heard

date:

words heard

date:

words heard

date:

date:

Open & Closed doors

God sometimes would use open and closed doors to direct our paths as we considered change.

I remember one time after my husband and I left our church that he was a pastor at, we weren't sure where God was leading us location wise.

We tried applying to every single job possible. Some of which were no brainers and were way over-qualified for but God kept all of those doors closed, despite our qualifications.

I mean, I'm talking pizza delivery jobs, and we are sitting here with Bachelor's degrees.None-the-less, God opened doors in the Cleveland area instead of the Ashland area and it was and is completely obvious that this is where He wanted us to end up!

Look at things in life that you ask God to open or close doors and when He does this, document it! All he asks of us is to put up our sails, He will put the wind in our sails to guide us to where we should go!

open & closed doors

date:

date:

date:

open & closed doors

date:

date:

open & closed doors

date:

date:

open & closed doors

date:

date:

open & closed doors

date:

date:

date:

open & closed doors

date:

open & closed doors

date:

date:

open & closed doors

date:

open & closed doors

date:

open & closed doors

date:

date:

open & closed doors

open & closed doors

date:

date:

open & closed doors

date:

open & closed doors

date:

open & closed doors

date:

date:

date:

open & closed doors

date:

open & closed doors

date:

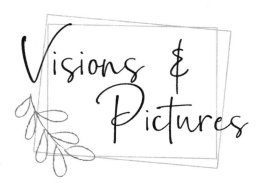

Visions & Pictures

I have had God give me pictures in my head but I used to always ignore these when I first would get them. I would dismiss them as non-sense or me not being able to focus. But when I started taking note of these, no matter how tiny, I started to realize that most of them actually meant something. If they didn't mean something to me, they meant something to another person.

I just started to be on the look out for them and take note of them all and sometimes I was even brave enough to ask if one came up during a prayer for someone - if it meant anything to them.

Sometimes it didn't and it took some pride to swallow that but when I would share pictures that did mean something....OHHHH the risk was it so worth it.

I think the biggest thing to remember is that hearing and encountering God has a lot of risk, risk of sounding stupid or being "weird" but the reward is so worth it. When you see others encountering Him and them experiencing how much God loves them, you can't get away from choosing that path.

Be brave. A lot of the time it's not even about you, it's about others that God puts on your heart.. And it's our duty and responsibility to help encourage them and connect their hearts with a Father that loves them.

visions & pictures

date:

visions & pictures

date:

visions & pictures

visions & pictures

date:

date:

visions & pictures

date:

visions & pictures

visions & pictures

date:

visions & pictures

date:

visions & pictures

date:

date:

visions & pictures

date:

visions & pictures

date:

visions & pictures

date:

date:

date:

visions & pictures

date:

visions & pictures

date:

visions & pictures

date:

date:

visions & pictures

date:

date:

visions & pictures

date:

visions & pictures

date:

visions & pictures

date:

visions & pictures

date:

visions & pictures

date:

visions & pictures

date:

visions & pictures

visions & pictures

date:

Miracles

This section, I honestly almost forgot about (hangs head in shame) but then realized, "What the heck, of course God is going to show up in Miracles!" I mean I've seen them in my every day life. Whether that be through friends who were told every day for 5 weeks while she was in the hospital trying to keep their baby in - that their baby had no chance of making it to an age where it could survive outside of the womb.

Every day the doctor came in with negativity, honestly, I'm sure to prepare the mother's heart for the loss but this mother knew her Daddy, her God - was stronger.

As weeks went by, the doctor, started coming in with disbelief that the baby was continuing to grow.

Her baby was born at 23 weeks and is now one of the chunkiest babies at over a year old. God is so good. (Yassss God - So happy for you TJ, Jacob and Baby Jacob!)

Miracles happen and we need to believe they can happen. Jesus said that we would be capable of even greater than He did here on earth - crazy right?!t - but let's start to expect them!

miracles

date :

miracles

date:

miracles

date:

miracles

miracles

date:

miracles

miracles

date:

miracles

miracles

date:

miracles

date:

miracles

date:

miracles

date:

miracles

date:

miracles

miracles

date:

miracles

date:

miracles

date:

miracles

date:

miracles

miracles

date:

miracles

miracles

date:

miracles

date:

miracles

date:

miracles

date:

miracles

miracles

miracles

miracles

miracles

date:

miracles

ERIKA JANE BAKER is a wife, mom of 3 under 5 and a Chief Operating Officer a multi-million dollar company. Erika was a pastor's wife for 5 years when her husband, Bryan, served as a Pastor in Ohio. After moving back to Erika's hometown, they started serving at a church where they lead a Missional Community that focuses on showing Jesus' love to those around them - where they live, work and play.

As they helped with different ministries within the church, they started to Encounter God speaking to them in different ways: through Sermons, Words Received, Journaling and more. As they pressed in, there was a sense of closeness they had never experienced with God. To the point that they started to see His character demonstrated day in and day out and they started calling Him, Dad.

Bryan and Erika's mission is to create safe spaces where people can Encounter their Dad. They don't claim to know everything nor be perfect but they do understand the transformational power of Encountering God and desire everyone to experience their Dad on their own as well. They pray this journal would be a catalyst to this encounter.

Made in the USA
Middletown, DE
22 December 2022

20162760R00186